THE PETE BUTTIGIEG COLORING BOOK

PETE FOR PRESIDENT

ILLUSTRATED BY
T. J. HAMPTON

Post Hill PRESS

A POST HILL PRESS BOOK
ISBN: 978-1-64293-539-4

Pete for President :
 The Pete Buttigieg Coloring Book
© 2020 by Post Hill Press
All Rights Reserved

Post Hill Press
New York • Nashville
posthillpress.com

Published in the United States of America

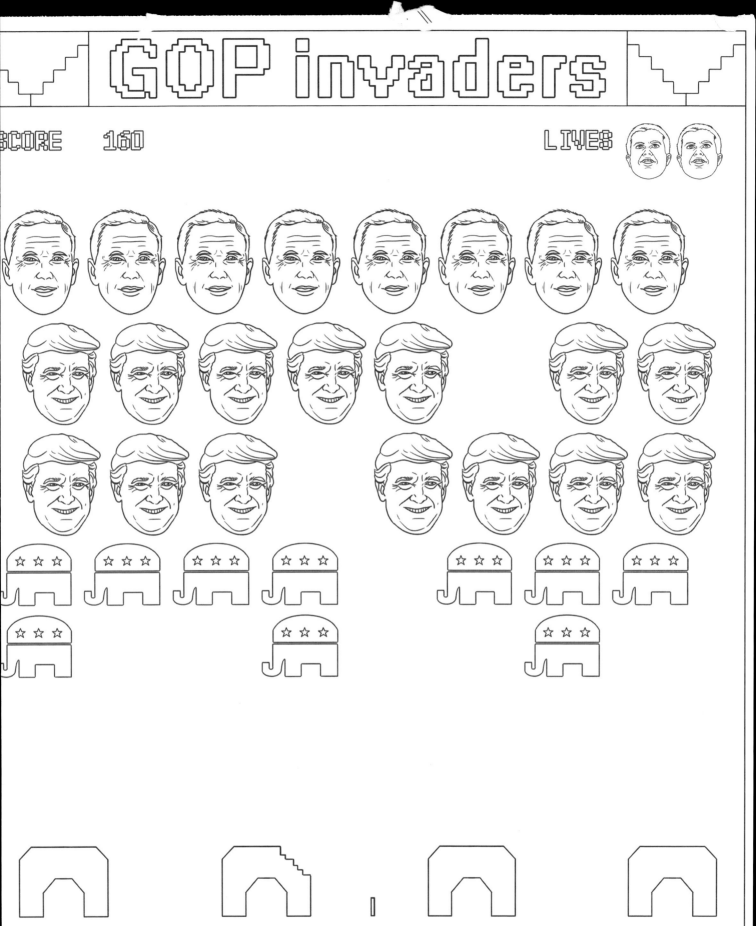
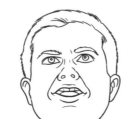

THE GREAT AMERICAN ELECTION SHOW